Decorative Quilting Patterns

45 Full-Size Designs

by Anne Szalavary

DOVER PUBLICATIONS, INC., New York

For Mom and Dad

Decorative Quilting Patterns: 45 Full-Size Designs is a new work, first published by Dover Publications, Inc., in 1989.

International Standard Book Number: 0-486-26001-1

Manufactured in the United States by Courier Corporation
26001103
www.doverpublications.com

Introduction

A quilt is made up of three layers—a top, often decorated with patchwork or appliqué; a lining, usually plain; and between them, a layer of padding for warmth. In order to keep the layers from shifting, and to keep the padding from forming lumps, some method of securing them is needed. In some quilts, this is accomplished by tying the layers together at intervals, but by far the most popular method is to stitch lines through the layers. Both the stitched lines and the process of making them are called *quilting*. Although the basic purpose of quilting is practical, it has developed into a highly decorative art. The quilting is an integral part of a quilt's design; indeed, many quilts have no decoration other than elaborate quilting. The 45 designs presented here can be used to fill in the plain areas of an appliquéd or patchwork quilt, or used alone to create striking quilts, wall hangings, pillows and other items.

General Instructions for Quilting

MATERIALS AND EQUIPMENT

Fabric

By the time you choose your quilting designs, you may well have completed your patchwork or appliquéd quilt top. If not, or if you are planning to use the quilting as the only decoration on your quilt, you should choose smooth, medium-weight, closely woven fabrics. Cotton has always been the most popular choice among quilters, but cotton/polyester blends may also be used, as long as the fabric is no more than about 65% polyester. Do not be tempted to use cotton sheeting for your quilt—it is so tightly woven that it is very hard to push the needle through it. For your lining, choose a fabric similar to the fabrics used in the top.

Batting

Throughout the history of quilting, various materials have been used as fillers for quilts—cotton, wool blankets, even straw. Today, the most widely used material is sheet batting. Many different types of batting are available, and each has its own characteristics.

Cotton batting, similar to that used in the majority of antique American quilts, will give the most traditional look to your quilted project; however, it is difficult to work with. It is very thin and tears easily; it also tends to shift and lump, so your lines of quilting need to be quite close together to hold it in place.

Bonded polyester batting is by far the easiest to work with, and is probably the most widely used. It is a very stable batting and does not need to be closely quilted, allowing for more "open spaces" in your quilt. Polyester batting comes in various thicknesses; the "proper" thickness to use depends on the effect you want to achieve. The thicker the batting you use, the puffier your quilt will be; the thinner the batting, the smaller your stitches and the closer together the lines of quilting can be.

One major drawback of polyester batting is that the fibers of the batting can work their way through the fabric to appear on the quilt top as fuzz. This problem, called "bearding," is particularly troublesome with dark fabrics and with fabrics that are not 100% cotton. New types of batting have been developed to minimize the problem, including some made with cotton/polyester blends.

Wool batting, a very warm batting, is thicker than cotton but, like cotton, needs to be closely quilted to keep it from shifting. It is less widely available than cotton or polyester.

Silk batting, a very soft, drapable batting, is a luxurious, if expensive, choice for fine quilted clothing.

Quilting thread

Thread made specially for quilting is stronger than regular sewing thread, and usually has a coating to help it withstand the friction of hand quilting. Cotton, polyester and cotton/polyester blend threads are all available. Try several types to determine which you like best. Regular sewing thread coated with beeswax may also be used for quilting.

Traditionally, quilting is done with white thread or with thread the same color as the fabric. However, this is by no means a hard and fast rule. Amish quilts, for example, were usually quilted with black thread, and you may choose whatever color you wish. Do keep in mind that your stitches will be more visible if you use contrasting thread.

Basting thread

Any strong thread that will hold up under the strain of being stretched in a frame may be used for basting. Use a light-color thread, since dark thread may leave a "shadow" on the fabric.

Needles

Quilting needles, called "betweens," are very short needles with small eyes. They come in sizes 7-10, with 7 being the largest. Try several sizes and choose the one you are most comfortable with.

Quilter's pins

These are long, very strong pins with plastic heads. They are used to attach the quilt to the frame.

Large safety pins

These can be used to attach the quilt to the frame.

Iron

Use a steam iron to press the quilt top and lining before assembling them.

Thimble

Even if you do not normally use a thimble for sewing, you

should wear one for quilting. Choose a thimble with a flat top rather than a rounded one. You might want to try one of the many special thimbles that have been developed for quilters. The thimble should be worn on the middle finger of your right hand if you are right-handed or on the middle finger of your left hand if you are left-handed. Some quilters also use a thimble on the hand that is kept underneath the quilt to keep their finger from being pricked. This is a matter of personal preference.

TRANSFERRING THE PATTERN TO YOUR QUILT TOP

After your quilt top has been completed, the next step is to transfer the quilting design to the fabric. This can be done in a number of different ways. Please note that all of the designs in this book have rows of concentric lines around the main motif. These are guidelines for "echo" quilting and need not be transferred to the fabric.

Tracing
The easiest way to transfer the design is simply to trace it to the fabric. This method works well if you are working with a light-colored fabric. Use a very sharp hard lead pencil or a Berol Verithin silver pencil to trace the lines.

For darker fabrics, you can construct a very simple light table as follows: Buy a large sheet of windowpane glass (or use a storm window); tape the edges so that you will not cut your hands. If you have a table with a removable leaf, take out the leaf and place the glass over the opening. Otherwise, balance the glass between two pieces of furniture (make sure that the glass is steady). Remove the shade from a table lamp and place it under the glass. Place a sheet of white paper over the glass to diffuse the light, then place the pattern on the glass with the fabric over it. The lines of the pattern should show through clearly.

Dressmaker's tracing paper
Designs may also be transferred with dressmaker's tracing paper. Use the lightest-color paper that will show up on your fabric. Place the pattern on the fabric right side up. Slip the tracing paper, colored side down, beneath the pattern; pin the pattern in place, being careful not to pin through the tracing paper. Go over the pattern lines with a sharp pencil. In order to save your pattern, you may want to trace it onto another sheet of paper and work with the tracing instead of the original.

Perforated pattern
One of the oldest methods of transferring designs is by using a perforated pattern. To do this, remove the pattern from the book. With a pin, needle or other sharp object, carefully pierce evenly spaced holes along the design lines. This can be done very quickly by sewing along the lines with an unthreaded sewing machine. Pin the perforated pattern to the fabric. To transfer the design to the fabric, rub a fine powder through the holes. The powder sold for use in hem markers can be used, or use talcum powder for dark fabrics and cinnamon for light. Remove the pattern and go over the lines with a hard lead pencil or a Berol Verithin silver pencil. Brush away the powder.

Template
For very simple designs, you can make a cardboard tem-plate. Cut the pattern out of the book or trace it. Glue the pattern to lightweight cardboard and cut exactly on the line (remember to ignore the echo quilting lines). Place the template on the fabric; hold it firmly in place and trace around it. Details can be drawn in freehand.

PREPARING TO QUILT

Once the quilting designs have been transferred to the quilt top, the top, batting and lining must be assembled. Unless you are planning to work on a full-size frame, the layers must be securely basted together to keep them from shifting.

Cut the lining 3″ to 4″ longer and wider than the quilt top, piecing the fabric if necessary. Press the lining thoroughly. Spread the lining, wrong side up, on a flat surface. Center the batting on the lining and carefully smooth out any wrinkles. Place the pressed quilt top, right side up, over the batting; smooth out any wrinkles. Starting in the center of the quilt, baste to the midpoint of each side, then baste from the center to the four corners. If your quilt is large, you may want to add additional rows of basting. For an alternate method of basting your quilt, work from the center out and baste horizontal and vertical lines across the quilt about 4″ apart to form a grid.

Some quilters recommend placing the quilt in a full-size frame to baste the layers together. It can then be removed from the frame and placed in a hoop or roller frame or quilted without a frame.

FRAMES AND HOOPS

Usually a piece to be quilted is placed in a frame or hoop to keep the layers taut as you work. A number of different frames and hoops are available, but they generally fall into one of three categories.

Full-size frame
A full-size quilting frame holds the layers of the quilt very securely and eliminates the need for basting. However, it takes up a great deal of room and its large size makes it unwieldy.

A simple full-size frame can easily be constructed from 1″ by 2″ pine boards and four 2″ C-clamps. Buy two boards 8″ to 12″ longer than the length of the quilt (the *stretchers*) and two boards 8″ to 12″ longer than the width (the *rollers*). For each board, cut a strip of heavy muslin or other fabric about 4″ wide and the length of the board. Fold the long edges of the strip to the center, then fold the strip in half with the edges inside. Place the strip on the board with the folded edge extending about ½″ over the edge. Using a staple gun, staple the strip securely to the board, placing the staples about 2″ apart. Mark the center of each roller.

Place four straight-back chairs where the corners of the quilt will be. Place the stretchers across the chairs with the fabric up and to the inside; place the rollers on top of the stretchers. Mark the center of the top and bottom edges of the lining. Spread the lining, wrong side up, over the frame. Matching the center marks, pin the center of the top and bottom edges of the lining to the fabric on the rollers. Now, working from the center out, stretch the lining toward the ends of each roller and pin it in place. Using quilting thread and a quilting needle, whipstitch the lining to the rollers or use large safety pins to attach the lining to the rollers. Clamp one of the rollers to the stretchers. Pull the other roller so that the lining is taut (this is much easier to do with two people); clamp it to the stretchers. Pin the side edges of the lining to the fabric on the stretchers.

Unroll the batting and spread it over the lining. Starting in one corner, align two adjacent edges of the batting with the edges of the lining, then smooth the batting out carefully. Trim off any excess batting.

Center the quilt top, right side up, over the batting and smooth it out carefully. Starting at one corner and working all the way around, pin it to the batting and lining every 2" to 3". Pull the quilt top taut as you pin, but be careful not to distort the blocks.

You are now ready to begin quilting. Quilt in as far as you can reach; unclamp one roller and unpin the lining from the stretchers at that end. Roll up the quilted portion, then reclamp the roller.

Roller frame

The roller frame is similar to the full-size frame, except that the stretchers are much shorter. It does not hold the quilt quite as securely as the full-size frame, but it has the advantage of taking up less room. The quilt layers must be thoroughly basted before being placed in the roller frame.

Whipstitch or safety pin the ends of the quilt to the rollers. Roll the ends of the quilt smoothly around the rollers, then clamp the rollers to the stretchers. Pin the side edges to the stretchers. Quilt the exposed area of the quilt; remove the pins and unclamp the rollers. Roll up the quilted area and unroll the unquilted portion; reclamp and continue.

Quilting hoop

A quilting hoop resembles a large embroidery hoop and is used in much the same way. Its major advantage is its convenience and portability. Baste the quilt layers together securely before placing your quilt in a hoop.

When using a hoop, always begin working in the center of the quilt. Smooth the quilt over the inner ring of the hoop. Place the outer ring on top and push it onto the inner ring. Tighten the clamp to hold the quilt taut.

THE QUILTING STITCH

The stitch used in quilting is a simple running stitch; however, working it through the three layers of the quilt requires special techniques. There are probably almost as many ways of working the stitch as there are quilters, and there is no one "right" way to do it. The methods described below work well for many quilters. Try them, as well as methods described in other quilting books, to see what seems most comfortable to you.

Pick a quilting line that will allow you to quilt toward your body. Thread your needle with an 18" length of thread; make a knot in the end. From the back, insert the needle into the lining about 1" away from where you want to start quilting. Bring the needle through the quilt top at the beginning of the quilting line. Tug gently, but firmly, on the thread until the knot pops through the lining and catches in the batting.

"Sewing" method

Place your left hand beneath the quilt (these instructions are written for right-handed quilters; if you are left-handed, reverse the instructions). Holding the needle perpendicular to the quilt or at a very slight angle, push it through the fabric with the top of the thimble until you can just feel the point

with your left index finger. To bring the needle back to the top, press the eye of the needle flat against the quilt with the thimble while pushing the tip of the needle up with your left index finger. With practice, you should be able to put several stitches on your needle before pulling it all the way through the fabric.

"In-and-out" method

In this method of quilting, only one stitch is taken at a time. It is slower than other methods, but it is extremely accurate.

Place your left hand (again, reverse the instructions if you are left-handed) beneath the quilt. From the top, insert the needle through the quilt with your right hand and pull it through with your left hand. With your left hand, insert the needle up through the quilt and pull it through with your right hand. Continue in this manner.

To end the quilting thread, take a small backstitch along the quilting line, then run the thread through the batting for about 1". Bring the needle out through the lining, pull the thread taut and cut it close to the surface. The end will disappear inside the quilt.

The ideal in quilting is to have very small, even stitches that are the same length on the back of the quilt as on the front; however, do not be discouraged if your stitches are larger than you would like. It is more important to have even stitches than to have small stitches. First work on making your stitches all the same length; with practice, you will be able to make smaller stitches.

FINISHING YOUR QUILT

After you have finished the quilting, take out all of the basting stitches and remove the quilt from the frame or hoop. There are several different ways of finishing the edges of your quilt.

Binding

If your quilt is rectangular, either straight or bias strips may be used for the binding; if the quilt has curved edges, you must use bias binding. Cut your binding strips about 1¼" to 1½" wide and join them to make a strip long enough to go around the quilt, plus 4" to 5" for corners and for overlapping the ends.

Trim the edges of your quilt evenly, leaving a ¼" seam allowance on all edges. With right sides together and raw edges matching, pin the binding around the quilt, mitering the corners and turning in and overlapping the ends. Stitch. Fold the binding over the edges of the quilt to the back. Turn in the raw edges of the binding and slip stitch it to the lining, covering the seam.

Self facing

If your lining fabric coordinates with your quilt top, you can fold it to the front to make a self facing.

Trim the quilt top and the batting even; trim the lining so that it extends ⅝" to ¾" beyond the top. Fold in ¼" on the raw edges of the lining, then fold it over the edge of the quilt to the front, mitering the corners. Slip stitch it in place.

Hemming

Trim the quilt top and lining even, allowing a ¼" seam allowance all around. Trim the batting ¼" smaller all around than the top and the lining. Turn in the raw edges of the top and lining and slip stitch them together.

Metric Conversion Chart

CONVERTING INCHES TO CENTIMETERS AND YARDS TO METERS

mm — millimeters   cm — centimeters   m — meters

INCHES INTO MILLIMETERS AND CENTIMETERS
(Slightly rounded off for convenience)

inches	mm		cm
1/8	3mm		
1/4	6mm		
3/8	10mm	or	1cm
1/2	13mm	or	1.3cm
5/8	15mm	or	1.5cm
3/4	20mm	or	2cm
7/8	22mm	or	2.2cm
1	25mm	or	2.5cm
1 1/4	32mm	or	3.2cm
1 1/2	38mm	or	3.8cm
1 3/4	45mm	or	4.5cm
2	50mm	or	5cm
2 1/2	65mm	or	6.5cm
3	75mm	or	7.5cm
3 1/2	90mm	or	9cm
4	100mm	or	10cm
4 1/2	115mm	or	11.5cm

inches	cm	inches	cm	inches	cm
5	12.5	21	53.5	38	96.5
5 1/2	14	22	56	39	99
6	15	23	58.5	40	101.5
7	18	24	61	41	104
8	20.5	25	63.5	42	106.5
9	23	26	66	43	109
10	25.5	27	68.5	44	112
11	28	28	71	45	114.5
12	30.5	29	73.5	46	117
13	33	30	76	47	119.5
14	35.5	31	79	48	122
15	38	32	81.5	49	124.5
16	40.5	33	84	50	127
17	43	34	86.5		
18	46	35	89		
19	48.5	36	91.5		
20	51	37	94		

YARDS TO METERS
(Slightly rounded off for convenience)

yards	meters	yards	meters	yards	meters	yards	meters	yards	meters
1/8	0.15	2 1/8	1.95	4 1/8	3.80	6 1/8	5.60	8 1/8	7.45
1/4	0.25	2 1/4	2.10	4 1/4	3.90	6 1/4	5.75	8 1/4	7.55
3/8	0.35	2 3/8	2.20	4 3/8	4.00	6 3/8	5.85	8 3/8	7.70
1/2	0.50	2 1/2	2.30	4 1/2	4.15	6 1/2	5.95	8 1/2	7.80
5/8	0.60	2 5/8	2.40	4 5/8	4.25	6 5/8	6.10	8 5/8	7.90
3/4	0.70	2 3/4	2.55	4 3/4	4.35	6 3/4	6.20	8 3/4	8.00
7/8	0.80	2 7/8	2.65	4 7/8	4.50	6 7/8	6.30	8 7/8	8.15
1	0.95	3	2.75	5	4.60	7	6.40	9	8.25
1 1/8	1.05	3 1/8	2.90	5 1/8	4.70	7 1/8	6.55	9 1/8	8.35
1 1/4	1.15	3 1/4	3.00	5 1/4	4.80	7 1/4	6.65	9 1/4	8.50
1 3/8	1.30	3 3/8	3.10	5 3/8	4.95	7 3/8	6.75	9 3/8	8.60
1 1/2	1.40	3 1/2	3.20	5 1/2	5.05	7 1/2	6.90	9 1/2	8.70
1 5/8	1.50	3 5/8	3.35	5 5/8	5.15	7 5/8	7.00	9 5/8	8.80
1 3/4	1.60	3 3/4	3.45	5 3/4	5.30	7 3/4	7.10	9 3/4	8.95
1 7/8	1.75	3 7/8	3.55	5 7/8	5.40	7 7/8	7.20	9 7/8	9.05
2	1.85	4	3.70	6	5.50	8	7.35	10	9.15

AVAILABLE FABRIC WIDTHS

25"	65cm	50"	127cm
27"	70cm	54"/56"	140cm
35"/36"	90cm	58"/60"	150cm
39"	100cm	68"/70"	175cm
44"/45"	115cm	72"	180cm
48"	122cm		

AVAILABLE ZIPPER LENGTHS

4"	10cm	10"	25cm	22"	55cm
5"	12cm	12"	30cm	24"	60cm
6"	15cm	14"	35cm	26"	65cm
7"	18cm	16"	40cm	28"	70cm
8"	20cm	18"	45cm	30"	75cm
9"	22cm	20"	50cm		

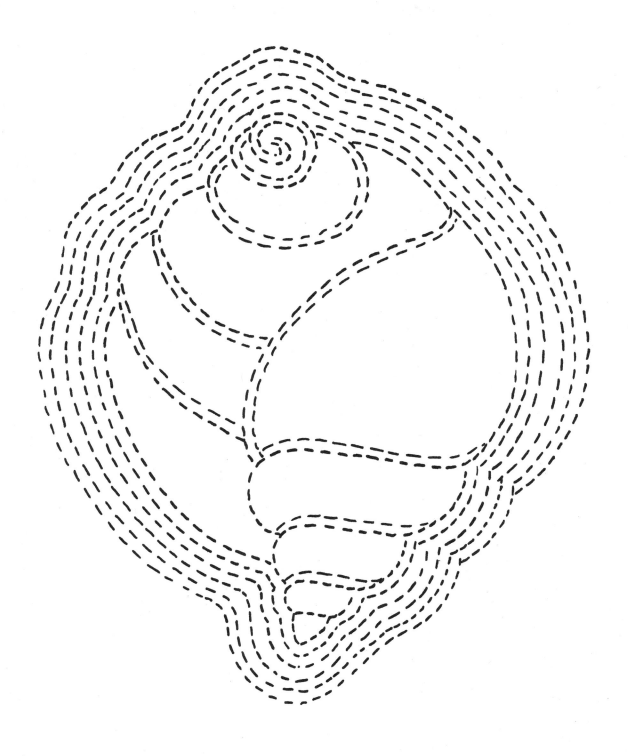

Plate 1

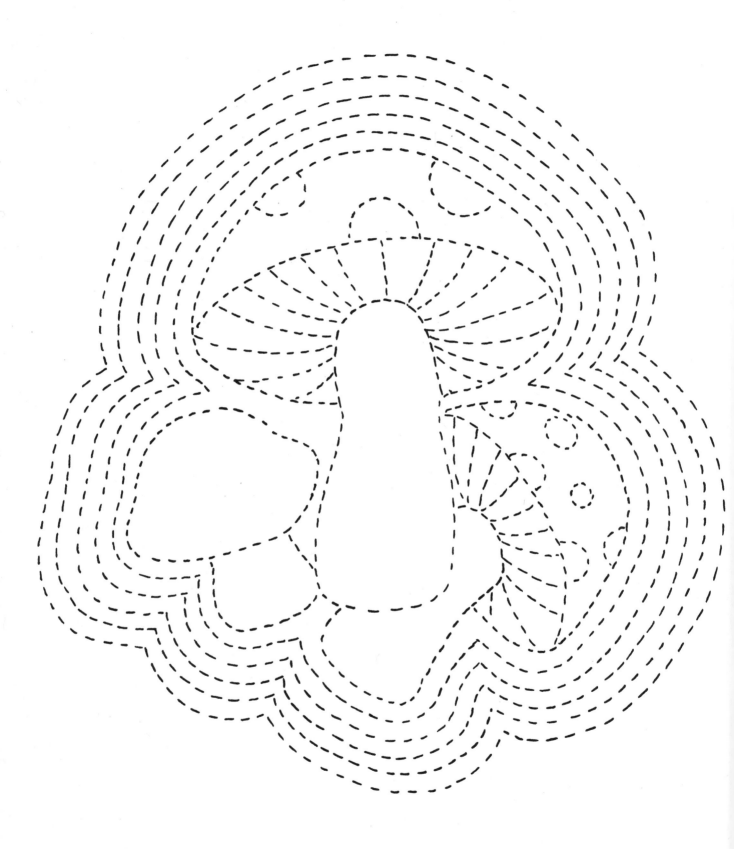

Plate 2

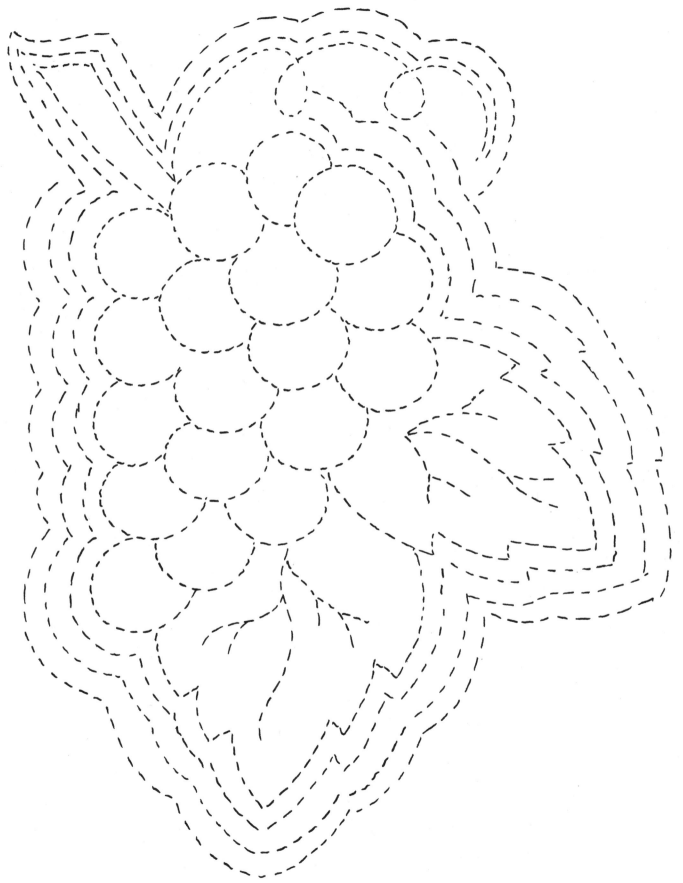

Plate 3

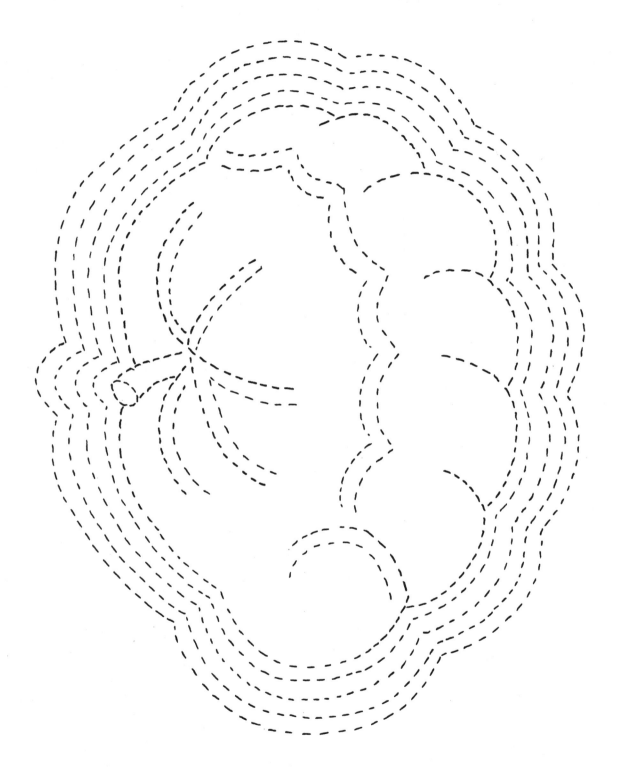

Plate 4

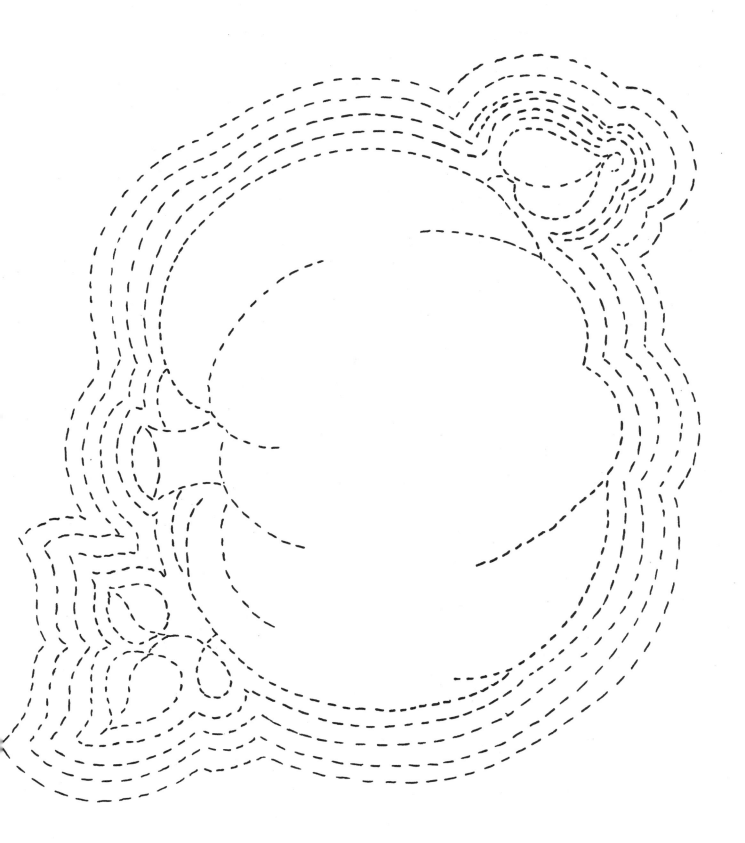

Plate 5

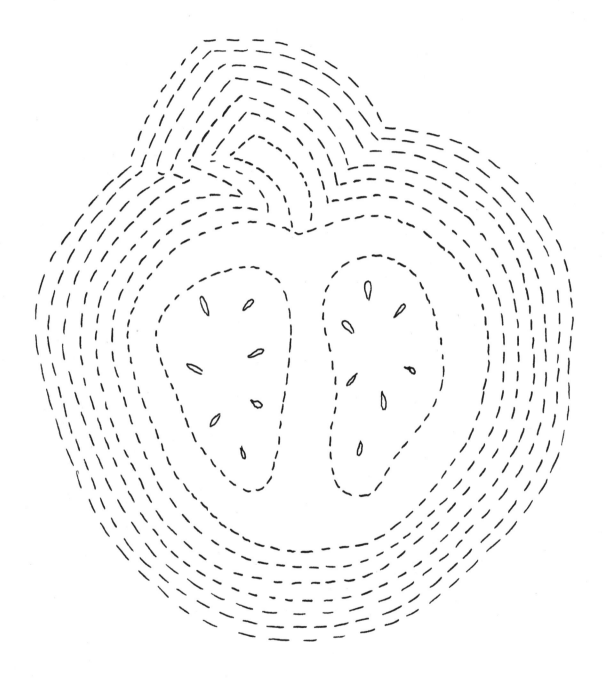

Plate 6

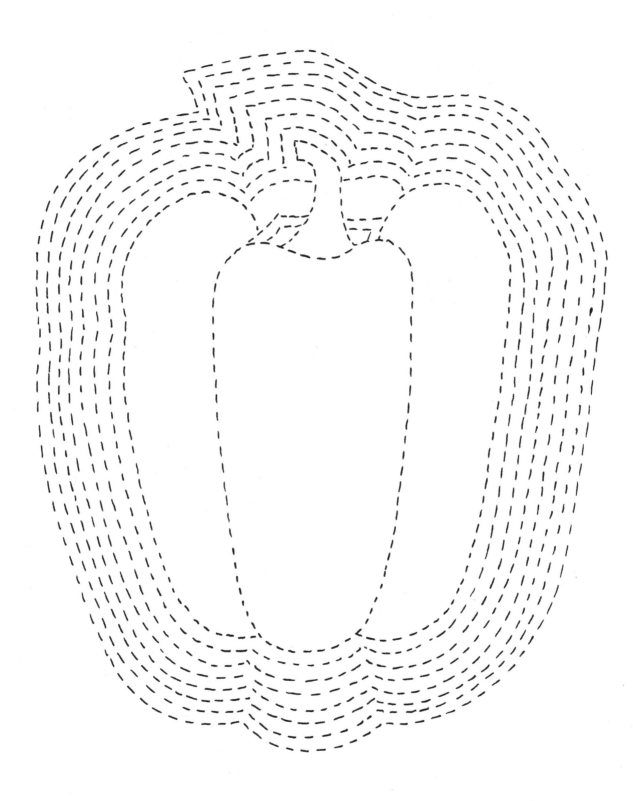

Plate 7

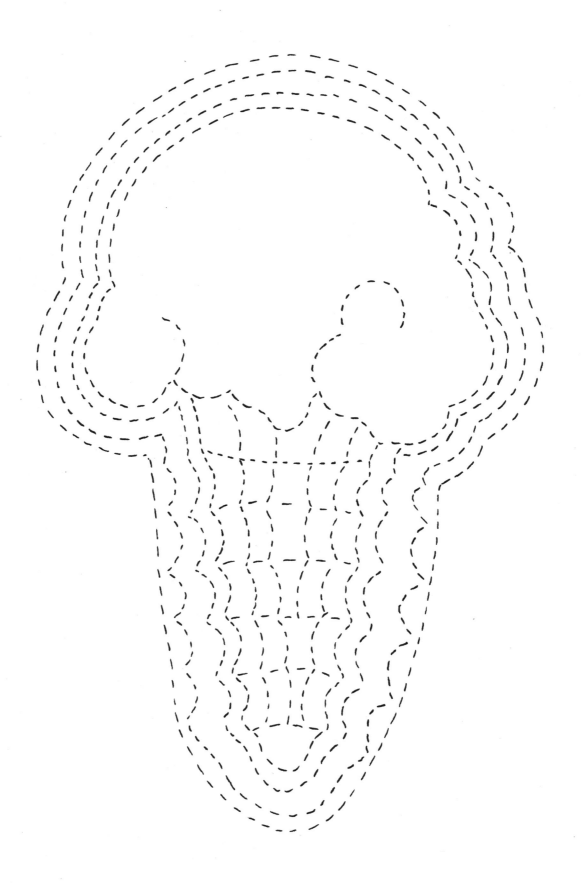

Plate 8

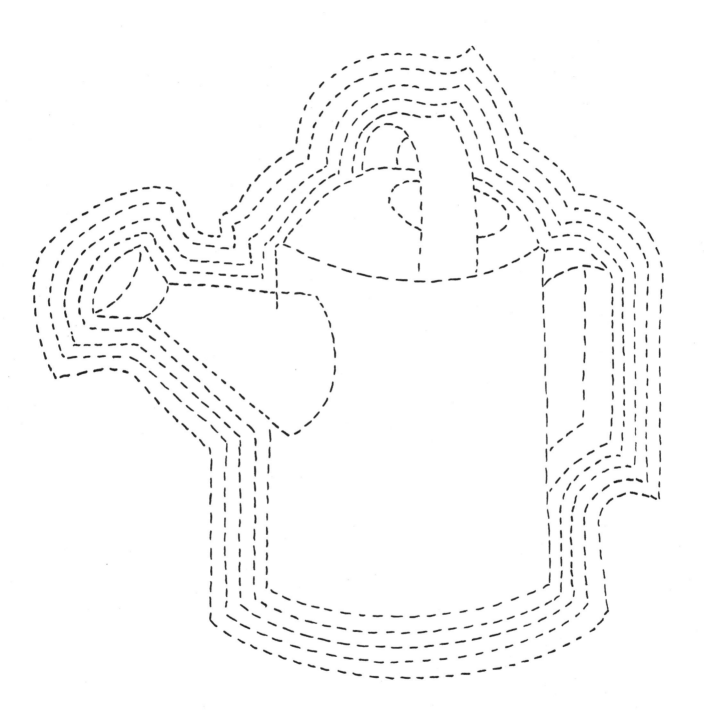

Plate 9

Charm Tacks

from THE Quiltmaker COLLECTION

Start

Charm Tacks

by Caroline Reardon

Combine quilting and tying and what do you have? Charm Tacks™! These little motifs, quilted in places where you would otherwise tie a quilt, are probably most appropriate for children's quilts, car quilts and sofa quilts. They add informal charm and personality to the surface of your piece. Since Charm Tacks have a casual "folk-art" look, if your quilting lines are a bit crooked or if two sides don't match perfectly, don't worry. That's how they are supposed to look.

Charm Tacks could be quilted by hand, but quilting them by machine is certainly the quicker and more durable choice.

In order to machine quilt, you need to drop the feed dogs on your machine (or cover them with heavy paper—like an index card—taped in place) so their action won't affect the movement of the quilt. You also need to use a darning foot rather than the regular presser foot on your machine. This way, you can move the quilt sandwich around under the needle in any direction while you are quilting.

If you are not already comfortable with machine quilting, practicing first on a small piece will help you get the feel of the "thread drawing" with stitches. Make a quilt sandwich large enough to become a big pot holder or small pillow. You may just like what you do right away and be able to use the piece in a practical way. Layer together a piece of lining, batting and top fabric, each about 12" square, and baste or pin it all together to make the quilt sandwich.

Remember how you used to draw stars on your papers at school? This is a very good motif for practice. First sew in one place for a couple of stitches and then slowly move the sandwich while you sew four or five tiny stitches; this will make the beginning "knot"—you know how hard these are to take out! Now thread draw the star, moving the sandwich in each of five directions until you are close to the beginning. Just before joining with the first stitch, again move the sandwich very slowly to end the line with very small stitches. Now, without cutting threads, move the sandwich to the next quilting site and begin again with short stitches. After quilting several motifs in an area, you can go back and trim connecting threads at one time.

Make several stars freehand until you get the feel of thread drawing. Then make up some simple shapes, ones that don't really look like anything, just needle doodles that help you practice drawing on fabric. These are your personal Charm Tack designs.

When you feel more comfortable with thread drawing, consider the various methods that follow for creating Charm Tacks on your quilt. For the motifs that have an opening in the design, begin machine quilting at the beginning of the line; this will enable you to complete the design in one continuous path.

Start

If you would like your quilted Charm Tack designs to look just like the motifs included here, there are several ways to do that.

• The time-honored way to recreate a quilting design is to trace the motif on fabric and then follow the lines when quilting. Trace motifs on your quilt top before layering it with batting and lining. If light-colored fabric will be quilted with Charm Tacks, place the quilting pattern under the fabric with a light source behind all layers and then trace the motif on the fabric. For both light and dark fabrics, tracing from a stencil pattern works well, which you can make with stencil plastic and a double-bladed X-Acto knife.

The following techniques are ways of marking the quilting motif *after* the quilt sandwich has been basted together.

First, stitch in the ditch between blocks, along sash lines and around major shapes within the quilt; then add the little quilted motifs in places where they can be seen. A good rule of thumb for polyester batting is to quilt (or tie, or use Charm Tacks) about every 4". This is approximately the area covered by your fist, so you have a ready-made guide right at your fingertips.

• With a marker, trace a design on tissue paper (a tissue-like paper made especially for quiltmaking works best). Pin this tracing to the quilt top and stitch along the lines, or somewhere

close. Then tear away the tissue paper. Use tweezers to remove stubborn shreds of paper that want to stick in sharp points and short stitches.

• Another way of marking the quilt design is to make a template of the motif from adhesive-backed plastic shelf paper. Trace the outer line of the quilting motif on the plastic paper with a permanent pen (back lighting helps here, too), and then cut it out along the drawn line. Place the template on the quilt top and quilt around it, allowing yourself the freedom to wander a bit if you'd like. The pattern can be removed and replaced several times before you'll need a new one. The inner lines of some motifs may need to be recreated "by eye" or with a second template.

Would you like to quilt these motifs without even marking them on your fabric? Place the image next to your machine for quick visual reference and begin. Since many designs are asymmetrical, your interpretation of them will be just as good as the original.

Machine quilters often use aids to help move the quilt sandwich around under the needle. You may want to use quilter's gloves, rubber fingertips or a hoop to guide your quilt.

After quilting a few Charm Tacks, you will probably be creating many designs of your own. Play with them, enjoy them, don't worry if they're not perfect. They're a quick and charming way to finish a quilt.

Start

Plate 10

Plate 11

Plate 12

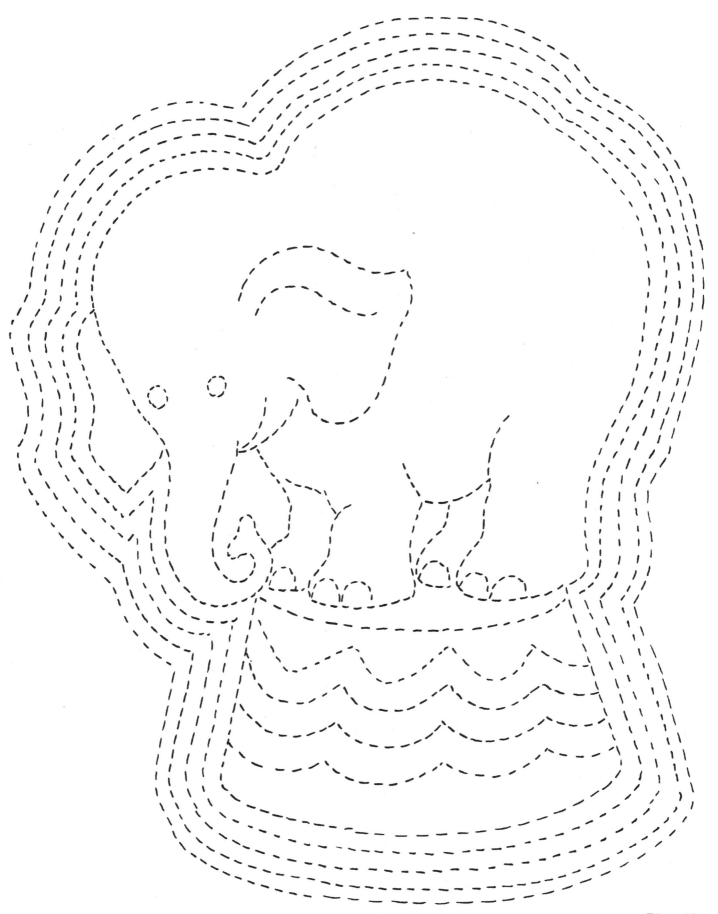

Plate 13

Plate 14

Plate 15

Plate 16

Plate 17

Plate 18

Plate 19

Plate 20

Plate 21

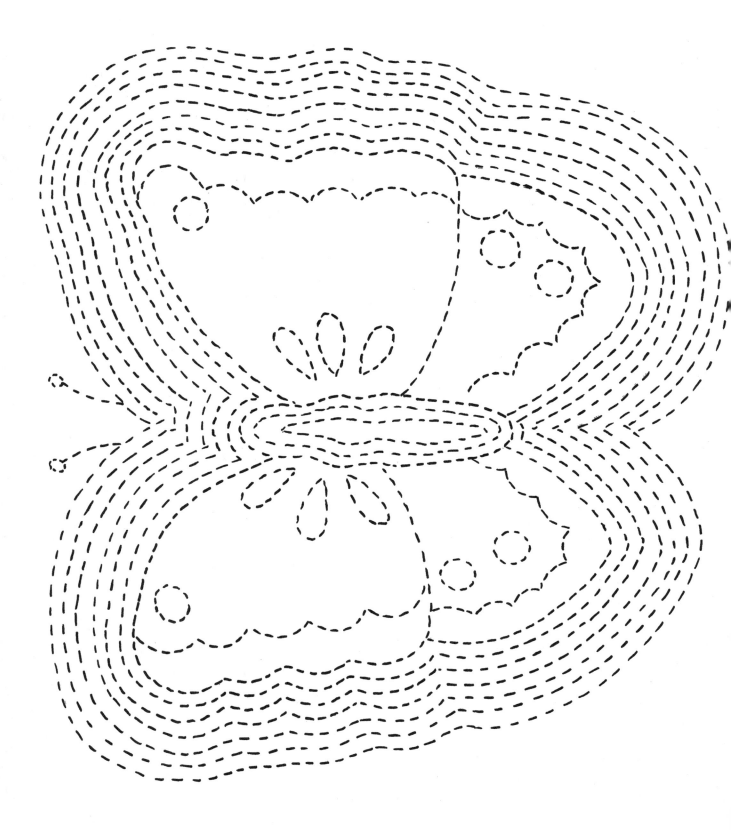

Plate 22

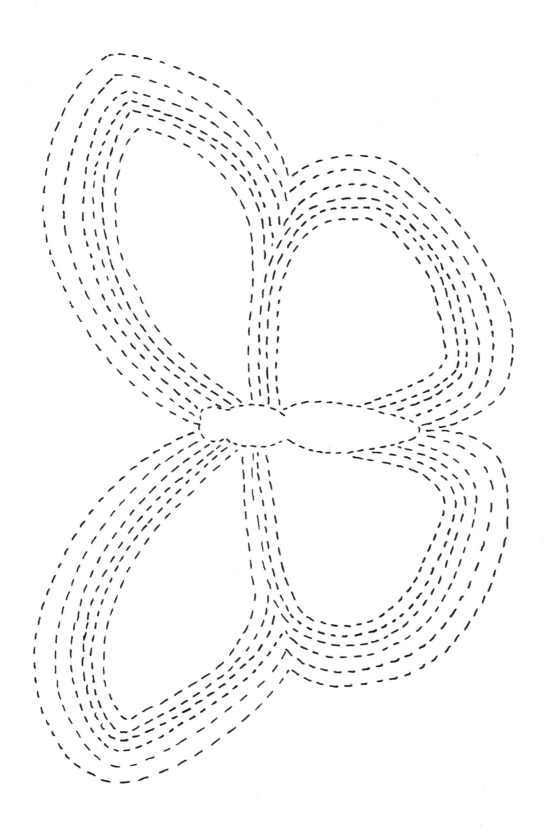

Plate 23

Plate 24

Plate 25

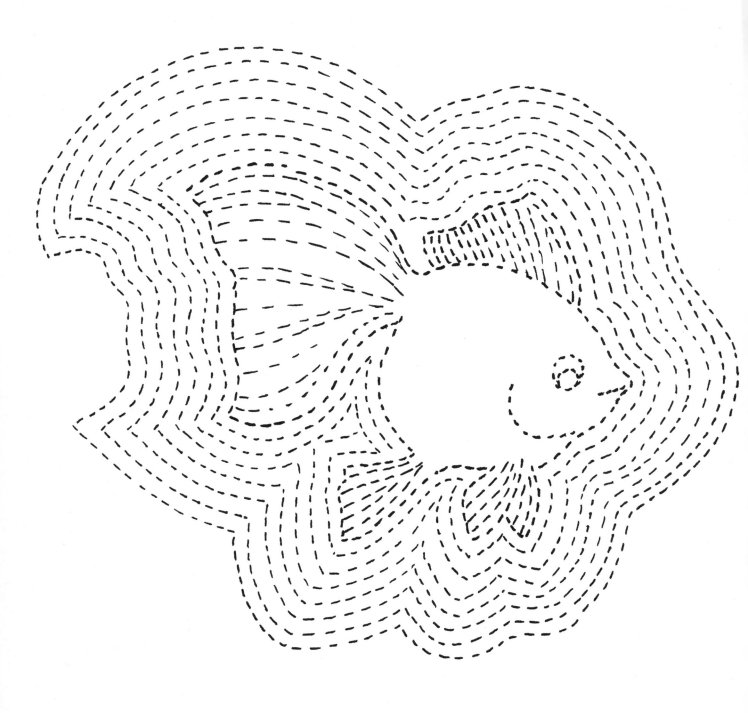

Plate 26

Plate 27

Plate 28

Plate 29

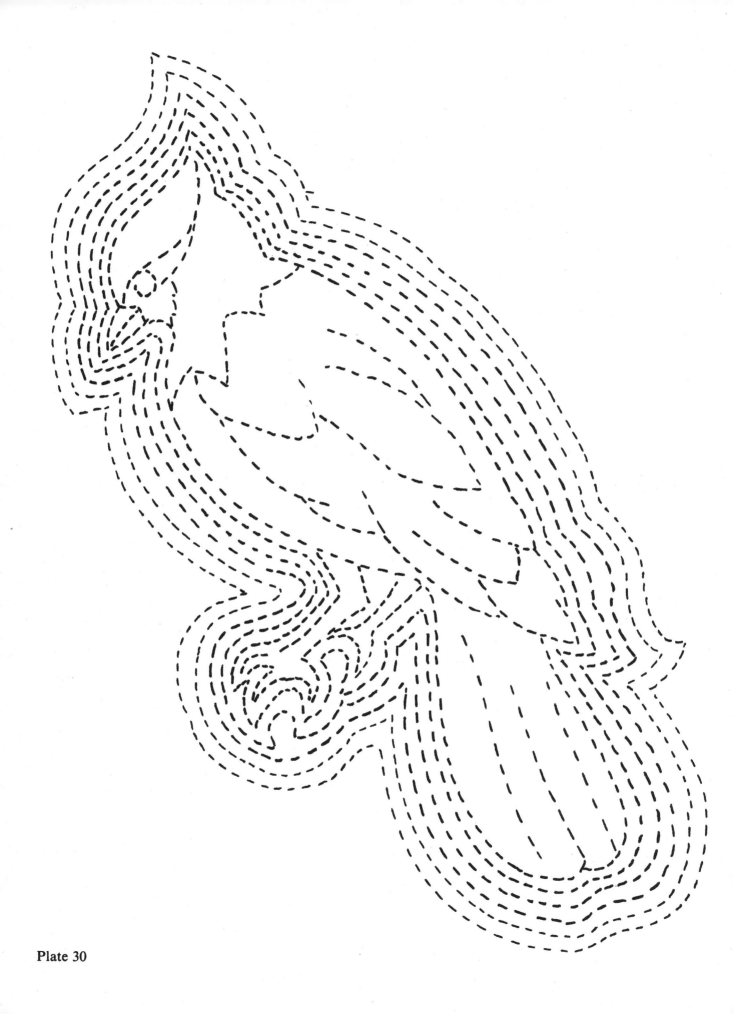

Plate 30

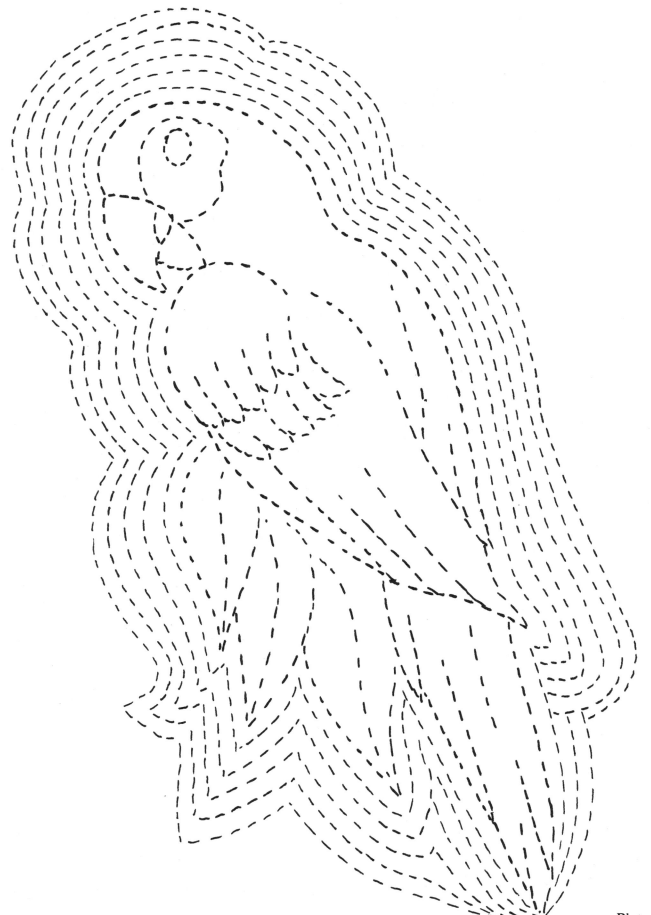

Plate 31

Plate 32

Plate 33

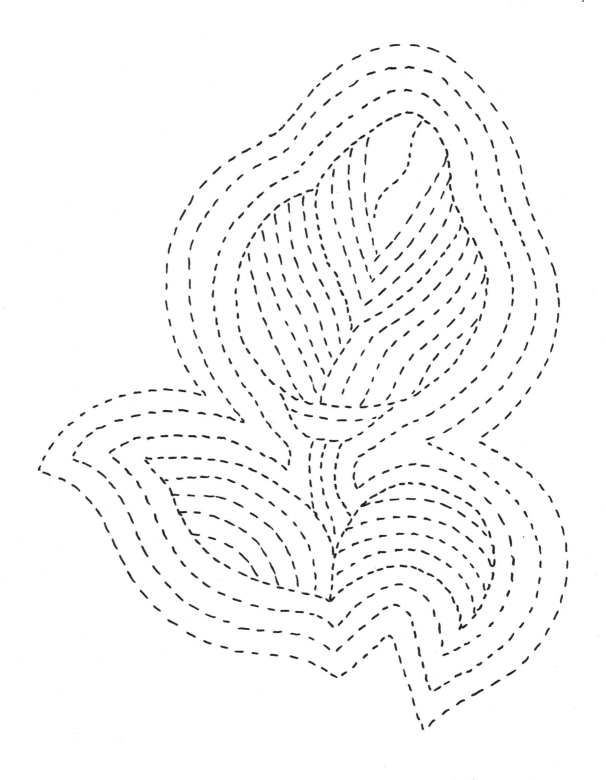

Plate 34

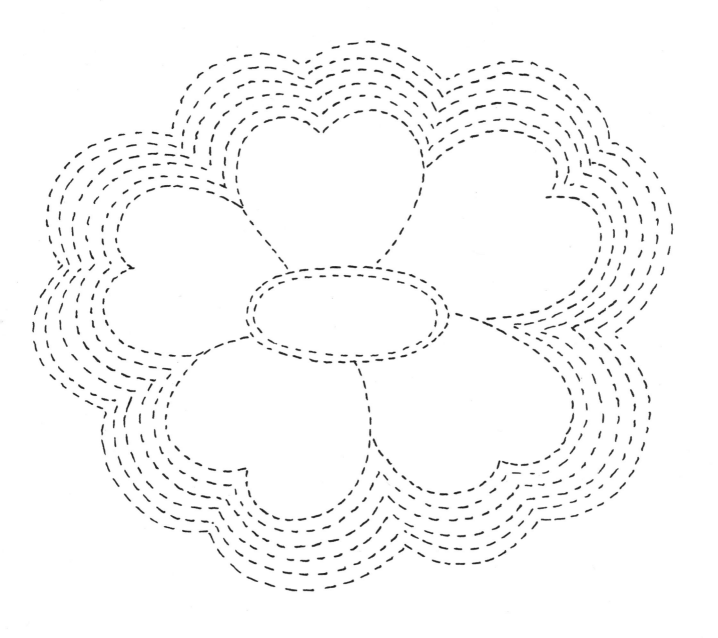

Plate 35

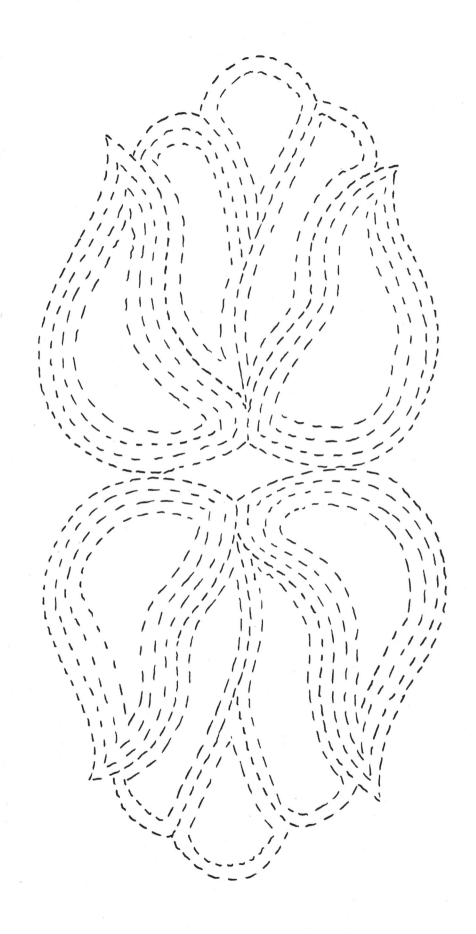

Plate 36

Plate 37

Plate 38

Plate 39

Plate 40

Plate 41

Plate 42

Plate 43

Plate 44

Plate 45